White

Blue

Usborne

First Coloring Book

Colors

Gray

Yellow

Orange

Red

Purple

Green

Pink

Brown

Black

This book belongs to

Tristan

Color the pictures and then add stickers.

In the sunshine

Yellow sun

Yellow bee

Purple butterfly

Brown shovel

Purple flower

Pink flower

Orange flower

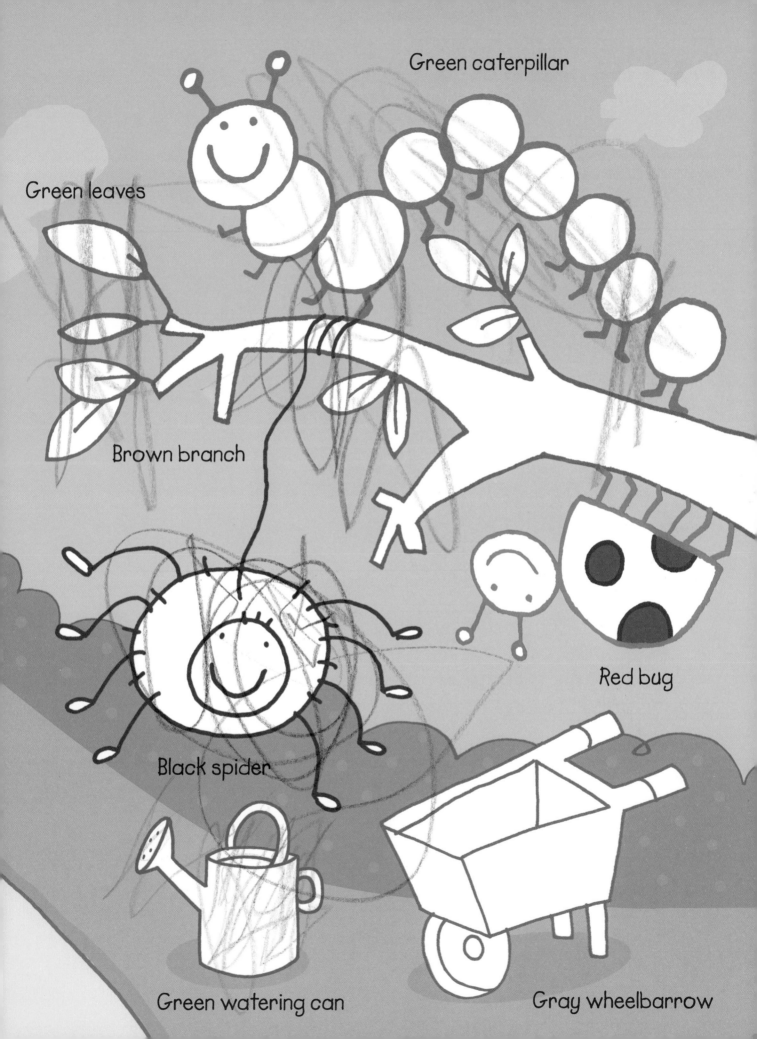

Green caterpillar

Green leaves

Brown branch

Red bug

Black spider

Green watering can

Gray wheelbarrow

At the party

Red balloon

Green balloon

Gray elephant

Blue hat

Orange cat

Yellow candle

Pink cake

Blue flag

Green flag

Red flag

Pink hat

Brown dog

Green present

Purple present

Yellow present

Blue present

Red present

On the move

Yellow sun

Green truck

Blue car

Gray steam

Red train

Blue wagon

Purple sails

Red flag

Pink car

Brown suitcases

Orange bus

Yellow wagon

Green wagon

Purple wagon

At the beach

Gray seagull

Yellow sun

Orange giraffe

Pink umbrella

Green bucket

Black and white zebra

Blue shovel

Yellow

Green

Orange

Purple

Pink

Red

Blue

Brown

Gray

White

Black

Gray elephant

Blue flag

Green sails

Blue surfboard

Yellow sandcastles

Red windmill

Purple ball

Pink shells

Green seaweed

Under the sea

Green seahorse

Purple octopus

Yellow fish

Green seaweed

Orange starfish

Pink shell

Orange fish

Blue shark

Black and white fish

Pink seahorse

Green seaweed

Red crab

Brown shell

On the farm

Yellow sun

Gray smoke

Red tractor

Black wheels

Brown scarecrow

Brown dog

Pink butterfly

Red boots

Purple wheelbarrow

Black wheel

Green tree

Red barn

Brown trunk

Black and white cow

Blue pond

Orange cat

Blue boots

Yellow chicks

High in the sky

Red balloon

Yellow moon

Yellow stars

Orange plane

Brown bird

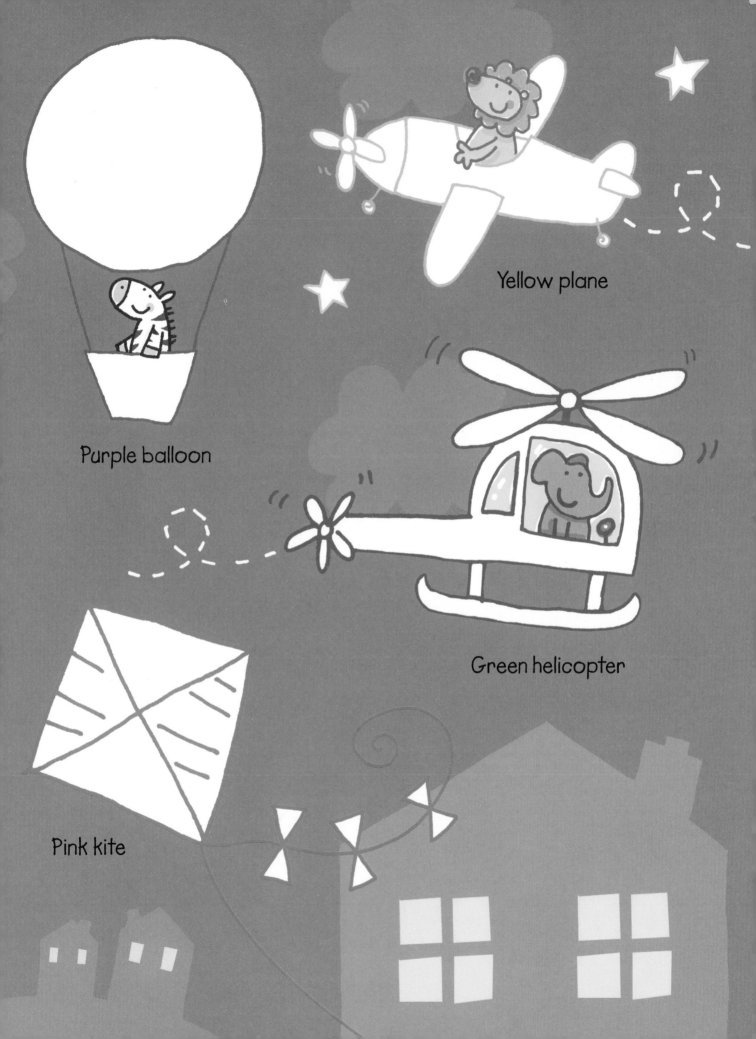

Purple balloon

Yellow plane

Green helicopter

Pink kite